Animal ABC!

By J. Douglas Lee

Pictures by Peter Woolcock

Gareth Stevens Publishing
Milwaukee

BRIGHT IDEA BOOKS:

First Words!
Picture Dictionary!
Opposites!
Sounds!

The Four Seasons!
Pets and Animal Friends!
The Age of Dinosaurs!
Baby Animals!

Mouse Count!
Time!
Animal ABC!
Animal 1*2*3!

Homes Then and Now!
Other People, Other Homes!

Library of Congress Cataloging-in-Publication Data

Lee, J. Douglas.
  Animal ABC!

  (Bright idea books)
  Bibliography: p.
  Summary: Illustrations and alliterative prose depict armadillos acting,
iguanas invading, and other active animals from A to Z. Includes special
activities encouraging the reader to respond creatively.
  1. English language — Alphabet — Juvenile literature. 2. Animals —
Juvenile literature. [1. Alphabet. 2. Animals] I. Woolcock, Peter, ill. II. Title.
PE1155.L43   1985   428.1 [E]   85-25144
ISBN O-918831-72-5
ISBN O-918831-71-7 (lib. bdg.)

This North American edition first published in 1985 by

Gareth Stevens, Inc.
7221 West Green Tree Road   Milwaukee, Wisconsin 53223, USA

Typeset by: Colony Pre-Press • Milwaukee, WI 53208 USA
Series Editors: MaryLee Knowlton and Mark J. Sachner
Cover Design: Gary Moseley
Reading Consultant: Kathleen A. Brau

Contents

aA

armadillos acting

4

b B

bears bathing

c C

cats crying

dD

dogs driving

eE

elephants eating

fF

foxes flying

15

g G

goats gardening

hH

hippos hurrying

19

i l

iguanas invading

21

j J jaguars jogging

k K kangaroos kicking

23

l L

lions laughing

m M

monkeys
making mischief

nN nightingales nursing

oO ostriches ogling

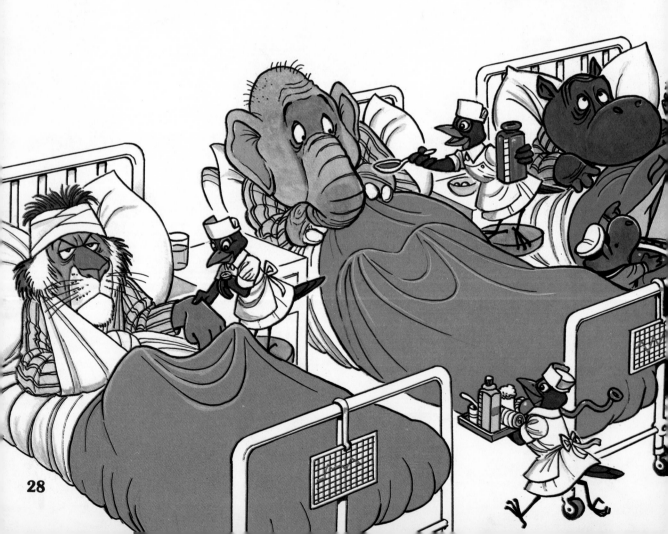

29

p P

penguins parading

q Q quails quivering

r R rabbits running

s S

squirrels storing

34

†T

tigers tobogganing

uU unicorns in uniform

vV voles visiting

w W

walruses washing

x X excited oxen

y Y yaks yelling

z Z zebras zig-zagging

43

Things to Talk About

The following "Things to Talk About," "Things to Do," and "New Animal Words" sections offer grown-ups suggestions for further activities and ideas to share with young readers of *Animal ABC!*

1. Look at the picture for the letter A (armadillos acting). How many times do you see the word armadillo in the picture? Do you know what an armadillo is? To find out what armadillo and other new words mean and how to use them, see the list of New Words.

2. Look for the words exit and acting on pages 4 and 5. Do you know what they mean? How can you tell what they mean from looking at the picture?

3. Look at the picture for the letter B (bears bathing). What words beginning with B can you use to describe some of the things you see in the picture?

4. Have you noticed that just about every picture in this book tells a story? Look at the following pictures, and think about or describe what stories they tell: * A (armadillos acting) *G (goats gardening) *M (monkeys making mischief) *S (squirrels storing).

Things to Do

1. Look at the picture for the letter <u>E</u> (<u>elephants</u> <u>eating</u>). Name as many things as you can that show up in the picture, besides elephants. See how quickly you can get a good idea of <u>everything</u> that is going on in this busy picture!

2. Pages 14 and 15 are called <u>foxes</u> <u>flying</u>. Think about the word <u>fox</u>.

   Now see how many words you can think of or write on a piece of paper that sound like, or rhyme with, <u>fox</u>. Ask a brother, sister, friend, or grown-up to add words to the list. One thing to remember: Words that <u>sound</u> like <u>fox</u> don't have to be <u>spelled</u> like <u>fox</u>.

New Animal Words

armadillo . . . . a mammal from South America with a covering like a suit of armor.
The armadillo now lives in the southern United States.

hippo . . . . the hippopotamus, which is a large land animal from Africa that spends most of its time in the water.
The photographer was surprised to find that a hippo can run faster than most people!

iguana . . . . a lizard from Mexico that lives in trees during the day.
The iguana is a fast runner, swimmer, and climber.

jaguar . . . . the only American big cat, yellow with black spots.
A jaguar can catch a fish by scooping it with her paw.

ostrich . . . . the world's largest bird, which lives in herds in open spaces.
The ostrich cannot fly, but it can run up to 40 miles per hour.

unicorn . . . . an imaginary animal that looks like a white horse with a twisted horn in the middle of its forehead.
People once believed that the horn of a unicorn had magic powers.

vole . . . . a rodent with longer fur and a shorter tail than a mouse.
A vole has tough teeth and eats bark from trees.

walrus . . . . a brown animal like a seal with tusks and whiskers.
An adult male walrus might be 12 feet long and weigh 3000 pounds!

yak . . . . a shaggy ox from Tibet.
The wild yak has long hair that sometimes drags on the ground.

More Books About Words

Here are some more books about words. Look at the
list. If you see any books you would like to read, see
if your library or bookstore has them.

ABC of Cars and Trucks. Alexander (Doubleday)

ABC of Children's Names. Ewen (Green Tiger Press)

A, B, See. Hoban (Greenwillow)

Alphabet Book. Eastman (Random House)

Animal Alphabet. Rebman (Green Tiger Press)

Animal 1*2*3! Lee (Gareth Stevens)

Bears' ABC Book. Wild (Trophy)

Christmas Alphabet Book. Whitehead (Troll)

Dr. Seuss's ABC Soup. Dr. Seuss (Random House)

Farmer's Alphabet. Azarian (Godine)

Find Your ABC. Scarry (Random House)

First Words! Lee (Gareth Stevens)

Guinea Pig ABC. Duke (Dial)

How to Write Codes and Send Secret Messages.
   Peterson (Scholastic Book Service)

Little Monster's Alphabet Book. Mayer (Golden Press)

Max's First Word. Wells (Dial)

My Word Book. Grosset & Dunlap (Grosset & Dunlap)

Opposites! Lee (Gareth Stevens)

A Phenomenal Alphabet Book. Edens (Green
   Tiger Press)

Picture Dictionary! Lee (Gareth Stevens)

Saying It Without Words. Esterer (Messner)

Secrets with Ciphers and Codes. Rothman (Macmillan)

Sesame Street Sign Language Fun. Bove (Random
   House/Children's Television Workshop)

Show of Hands: Say It in Sign Language. Sullivan and
   Bourke (Harper & Row)

Sounds! Lee (Gareth Stevens)

Teddy Bear ABC. Johnson (Green Tiger Press)

What's That You Said?: How Words Change. Weiss
   (Harcourt Brace Jovanovich)

When Will I Read? Cohen (Dell)

Word Works: Why the Alphabet Is a Kid's Best Friend.
   Kaye (Little, Brown)

For Grown-ups

Animal ABC! is a picture book that uses alliteration, lively illustrations, and easy-to-read prose to teach word and alphabet concepts and to encourage children to make up their own stories. The controlled vocabulary text (pages 4-43) complements and challenges a young reader's developing reading and language skills.

The editors invite interested adults to examine the grade level estimate below. Certain books lend themselves to reading level analyses using standard reading tests. *Animal ABC!,* because of its format, does not. This concept book helps children discriminate among objects by size, color, shape, and placement within the alphabet. The reading level of *Animal ABC!* is therefore determined not only by how "hard" the words are, but by a child's ability to grasp the subject matter in a visual format.

The grade span below reflects our critical judgment about the appropriate level at which children find the subject matter an achievable challenge.

Estimated reading level: Grade level 2-4